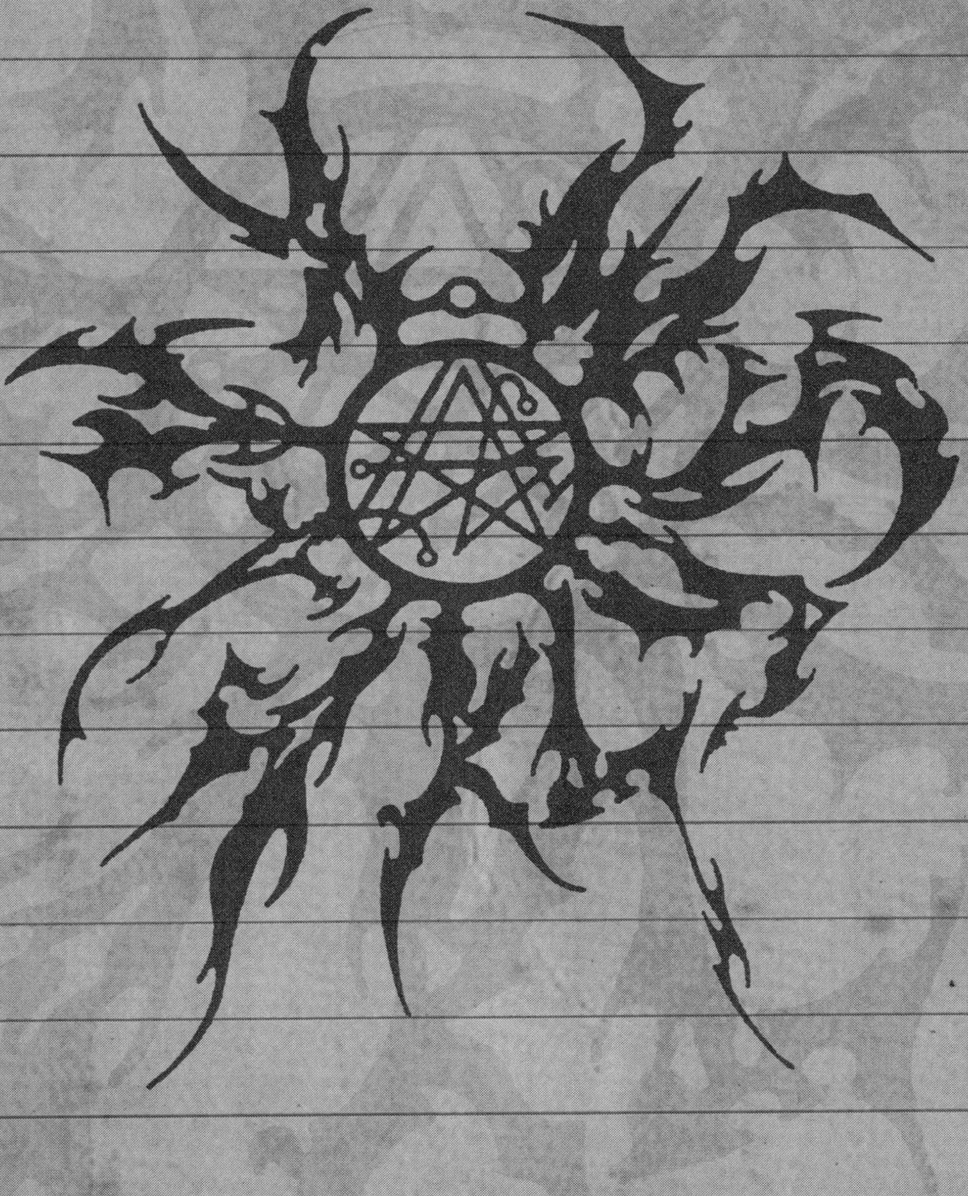

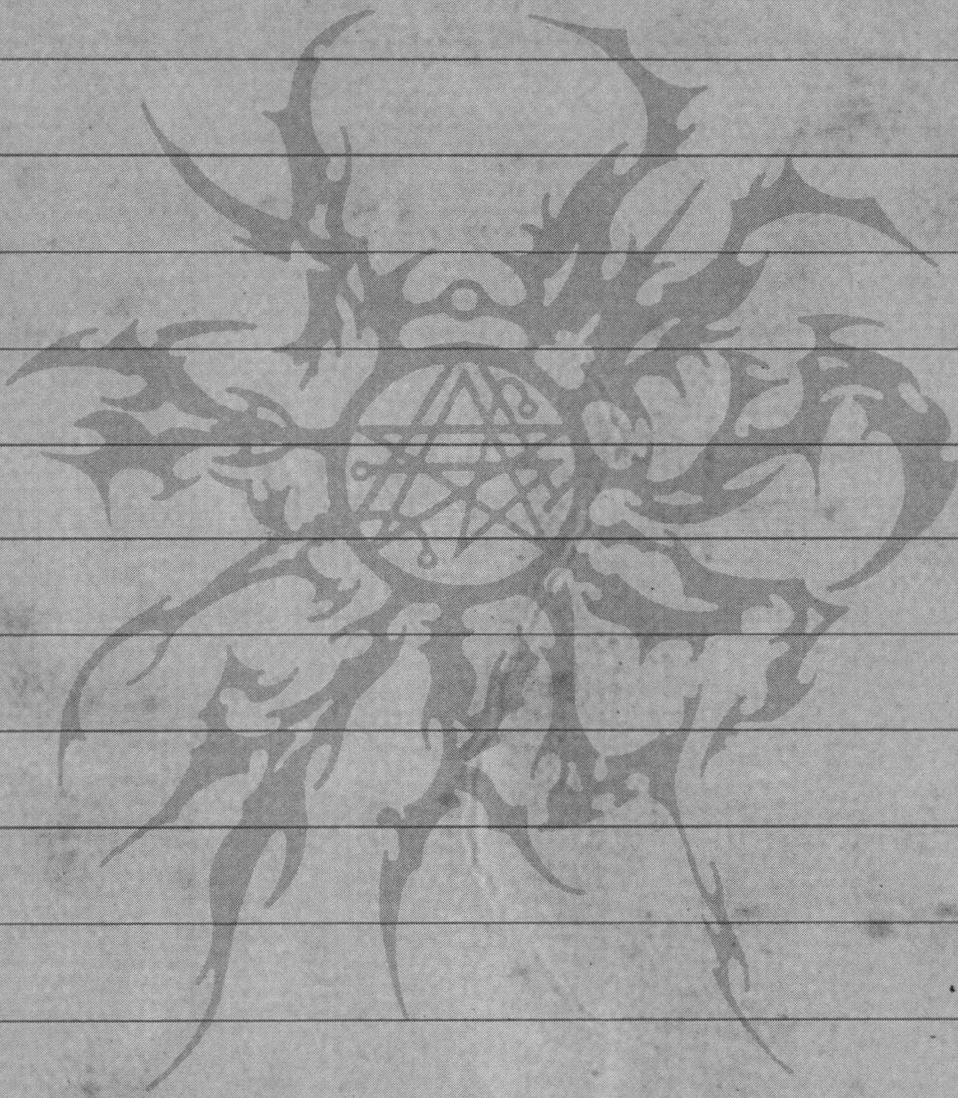

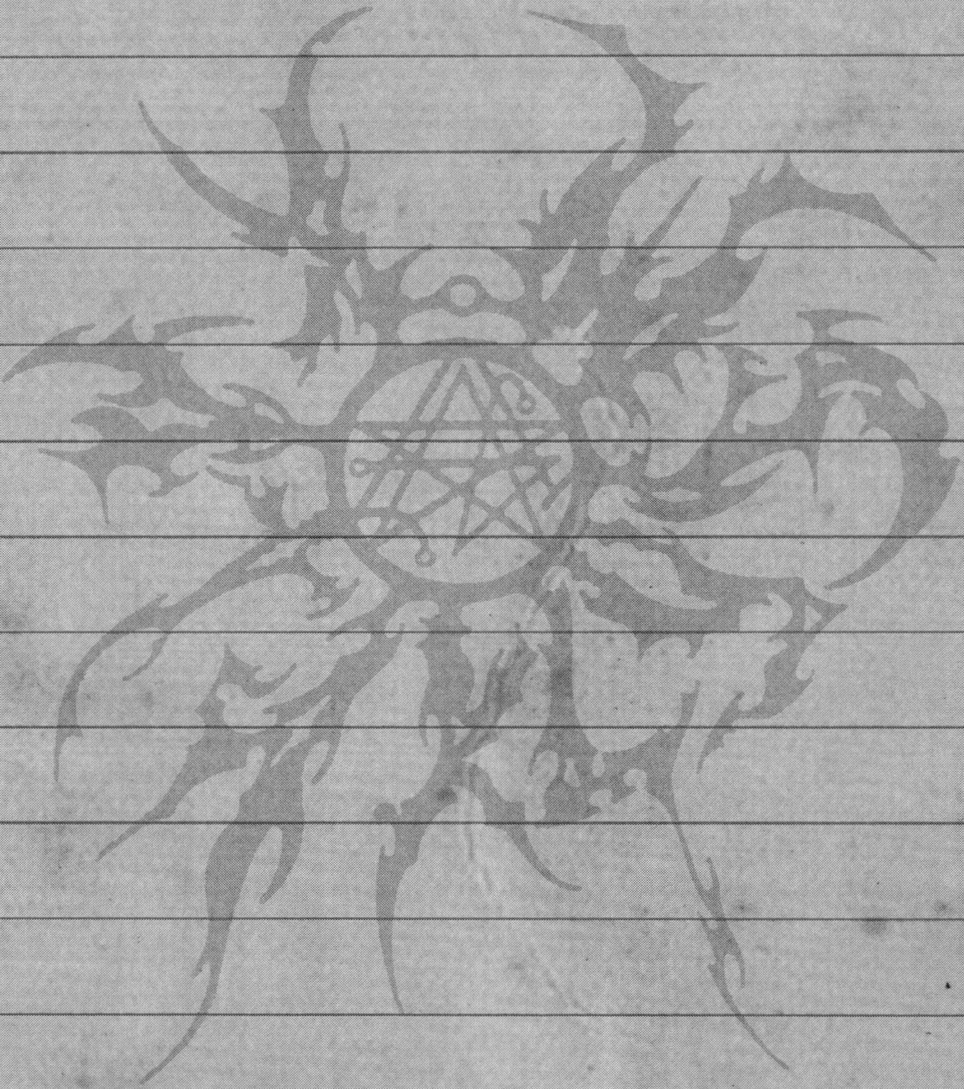

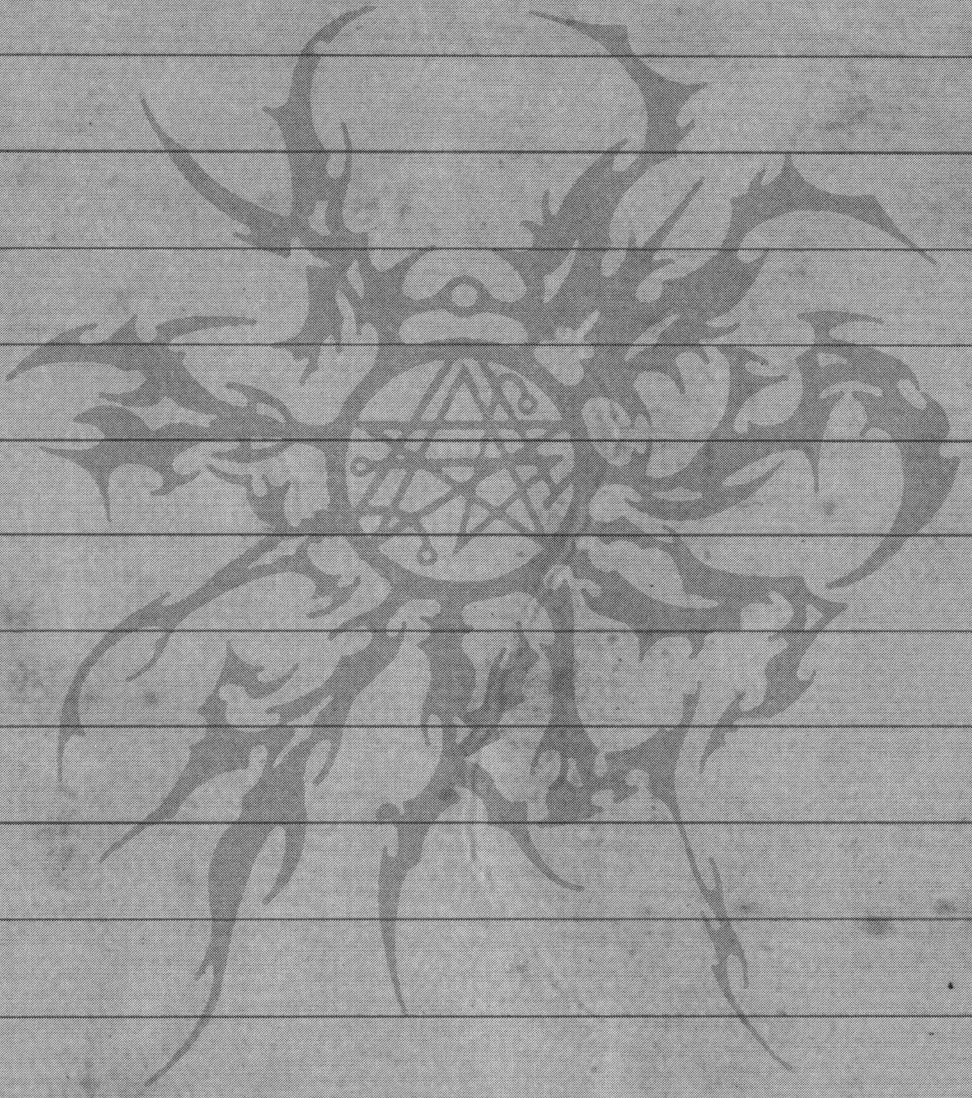

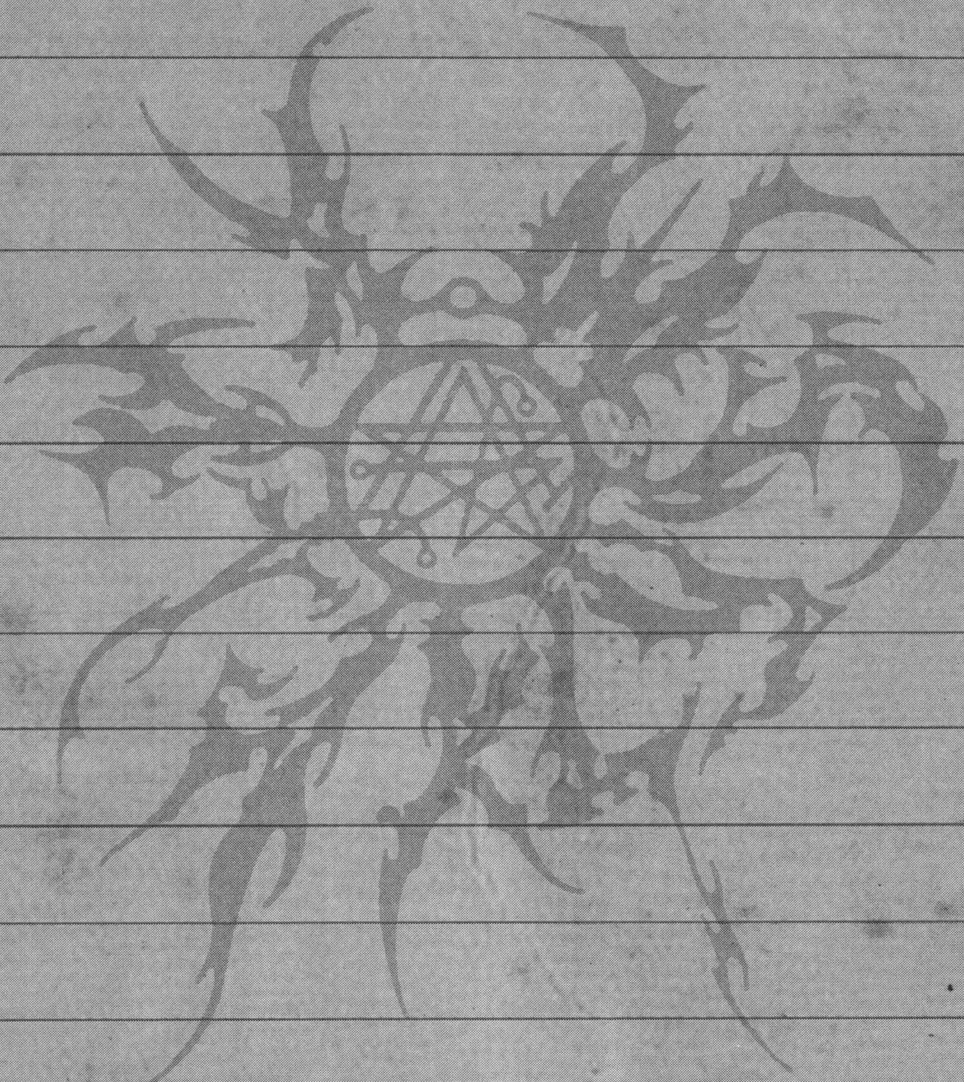

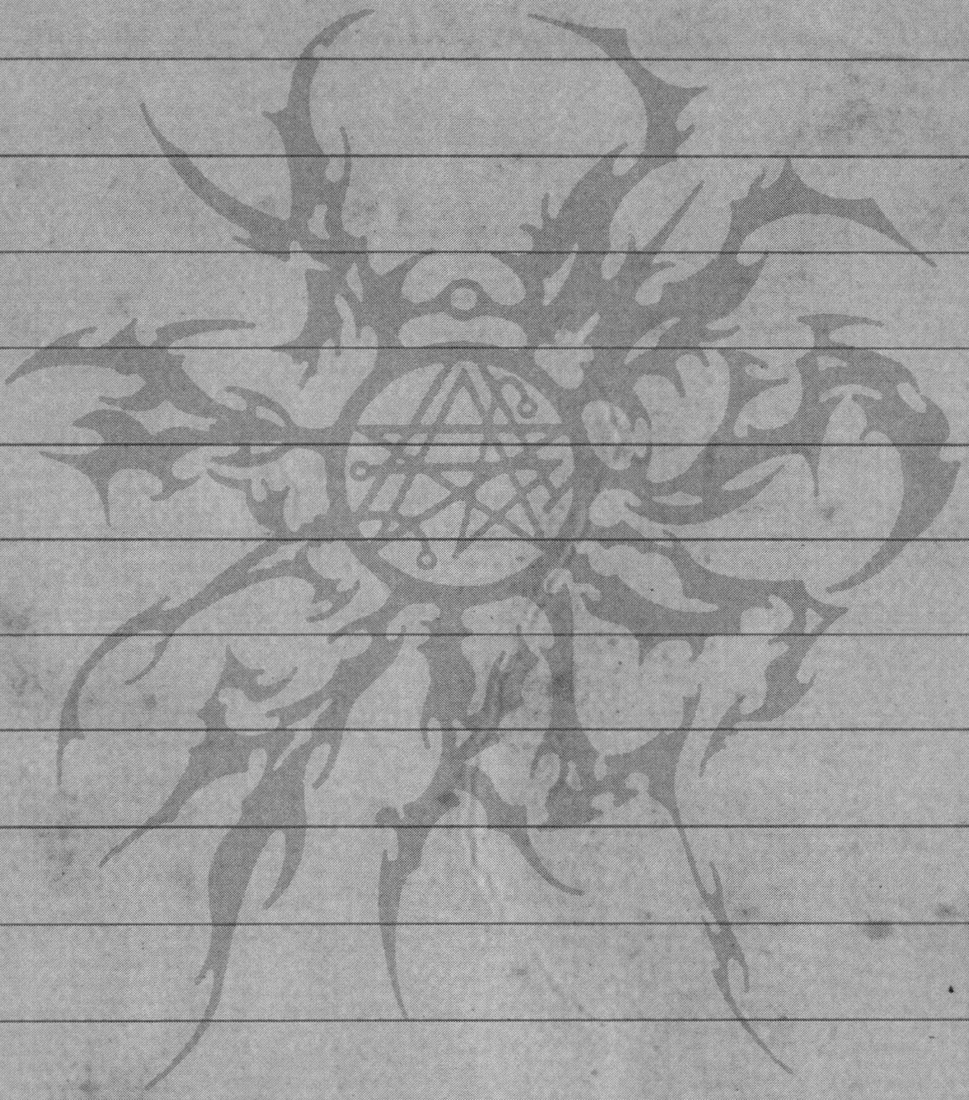

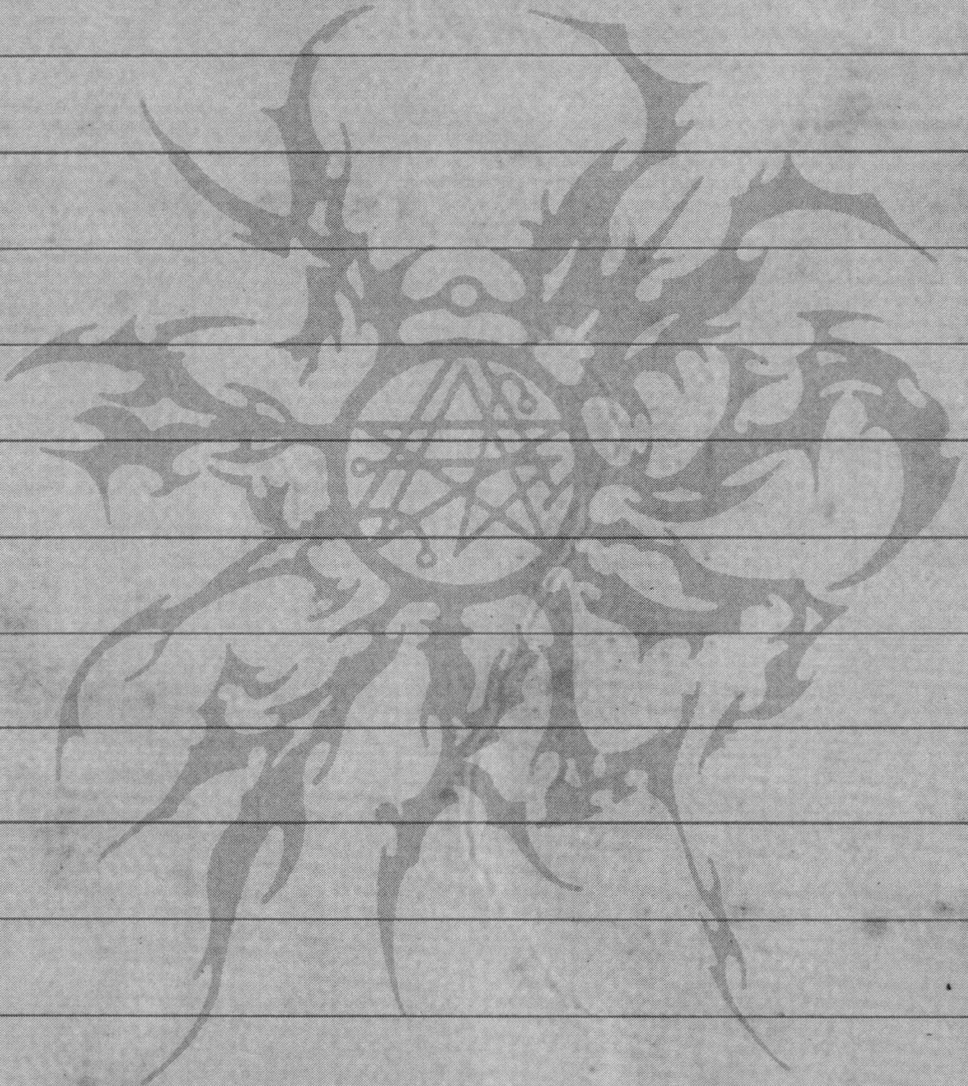

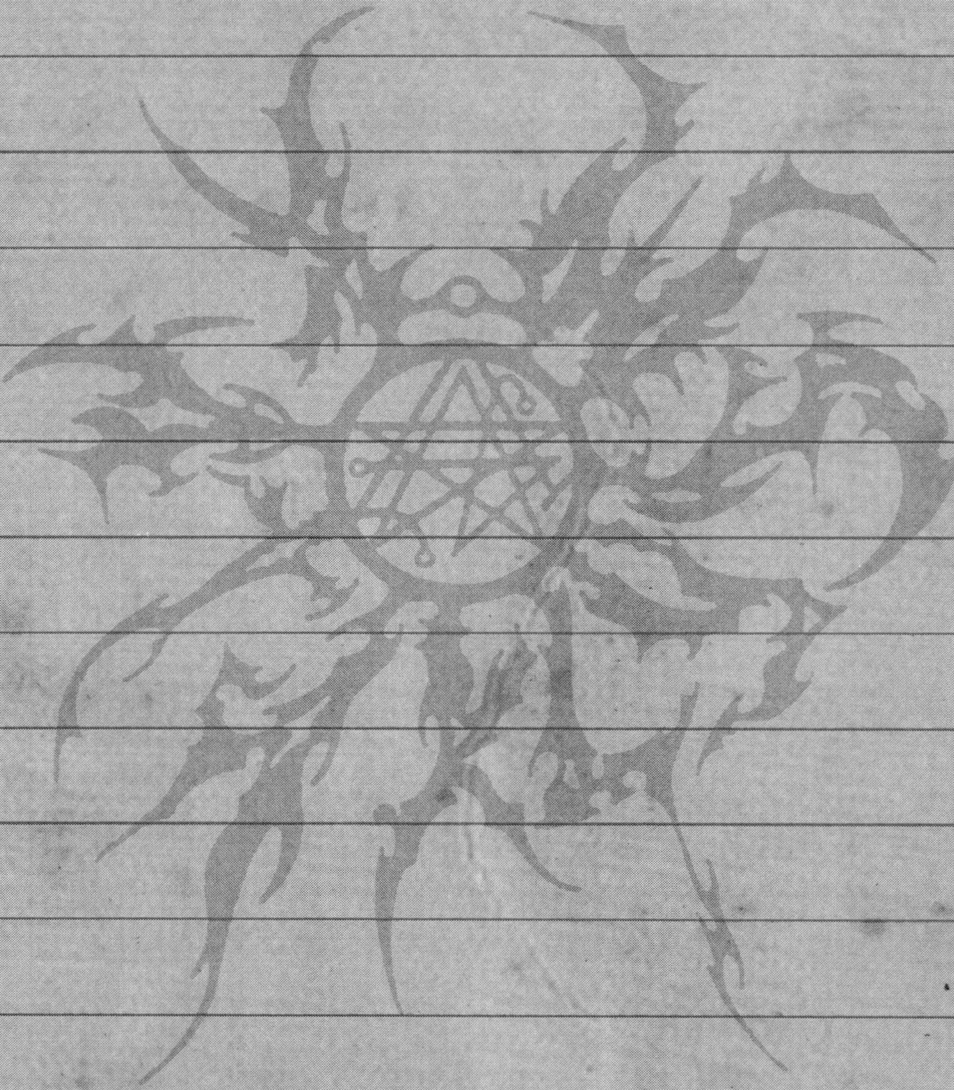

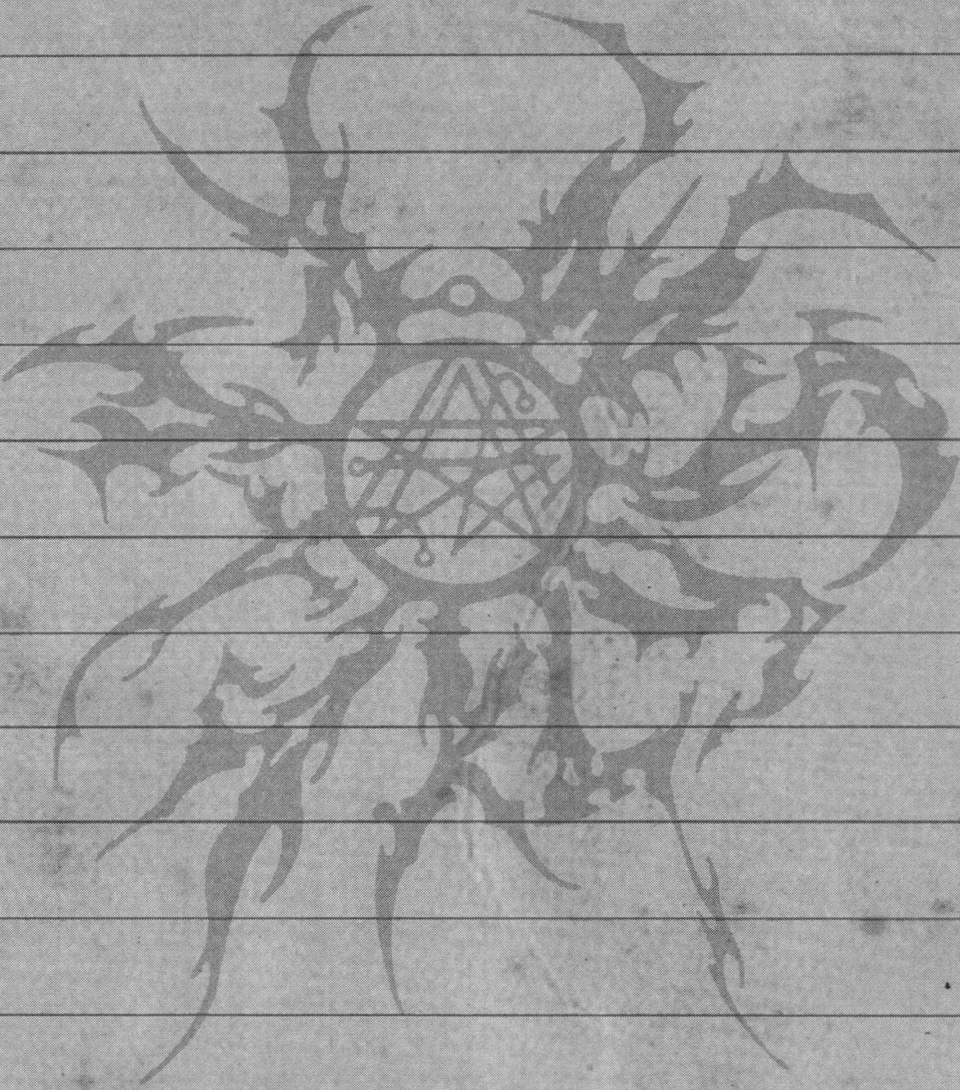

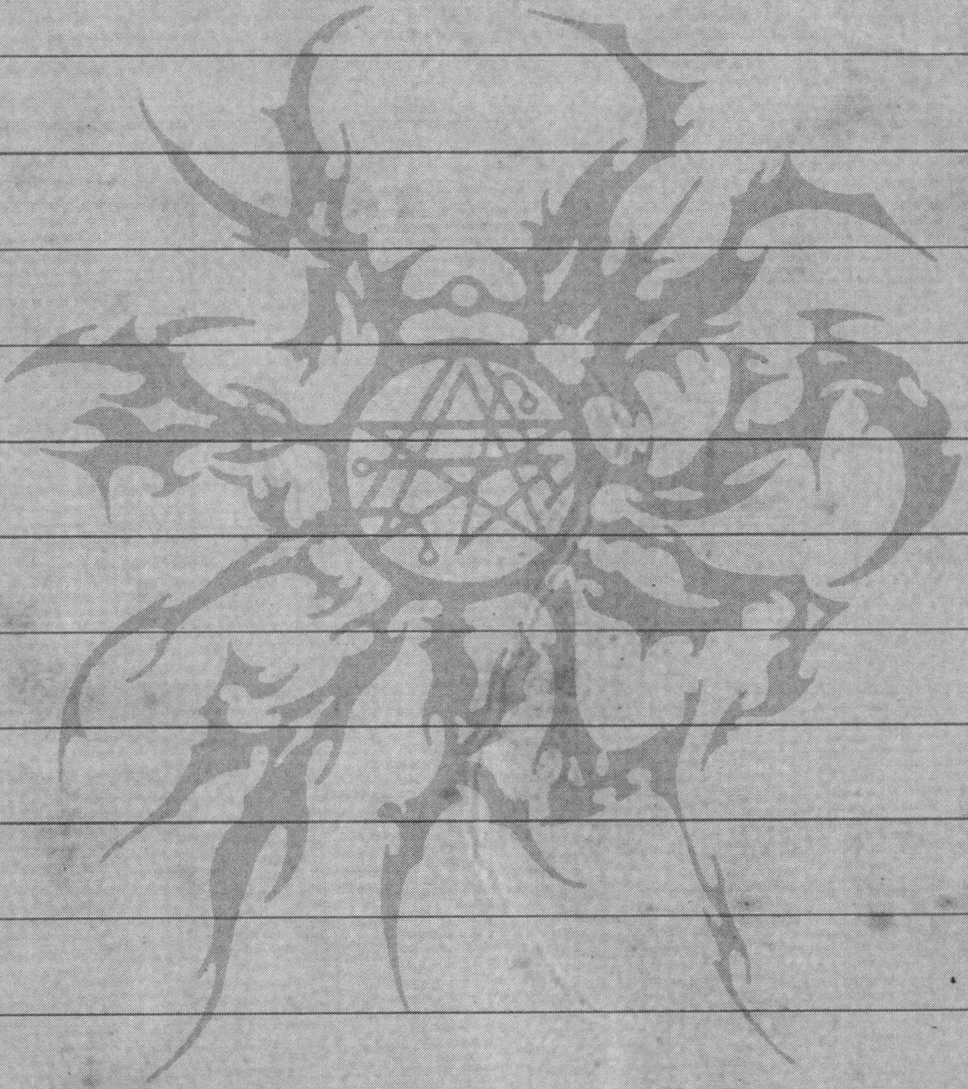

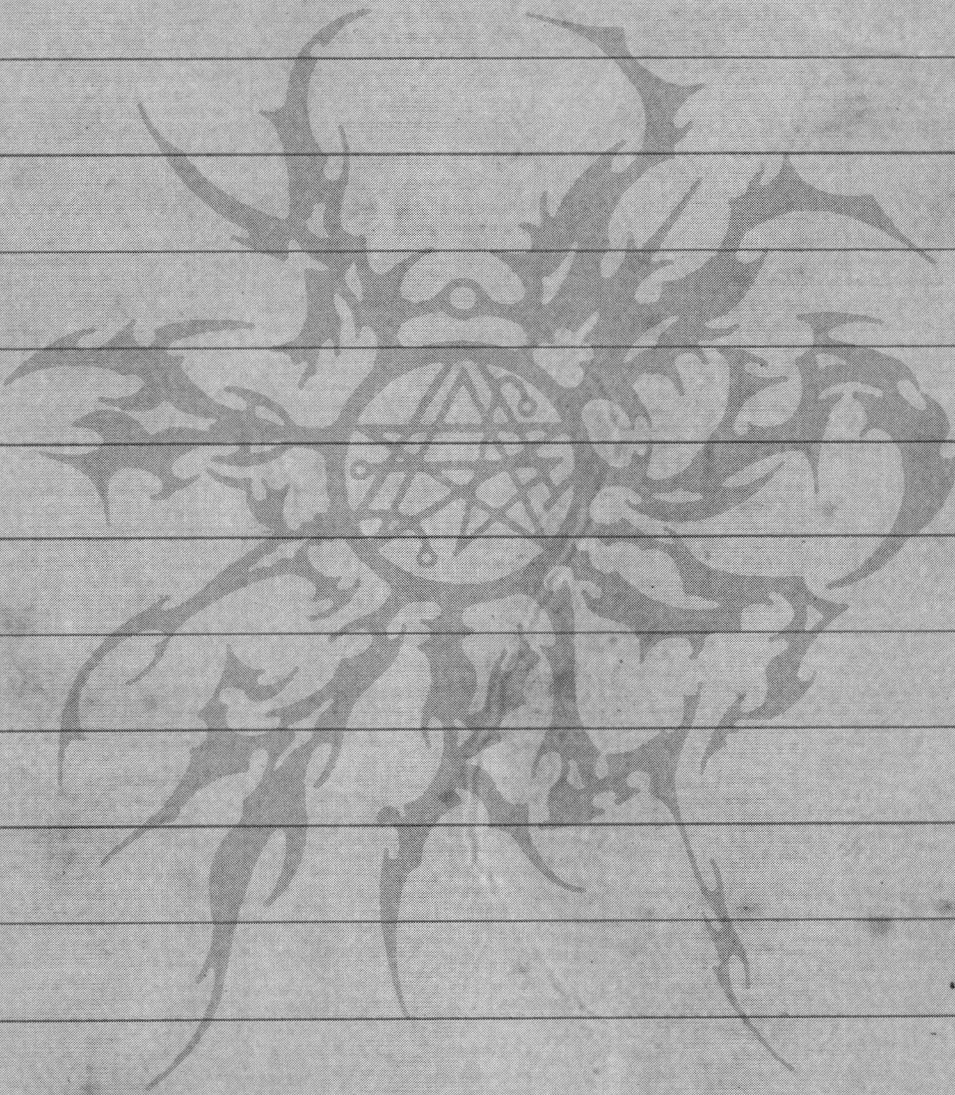

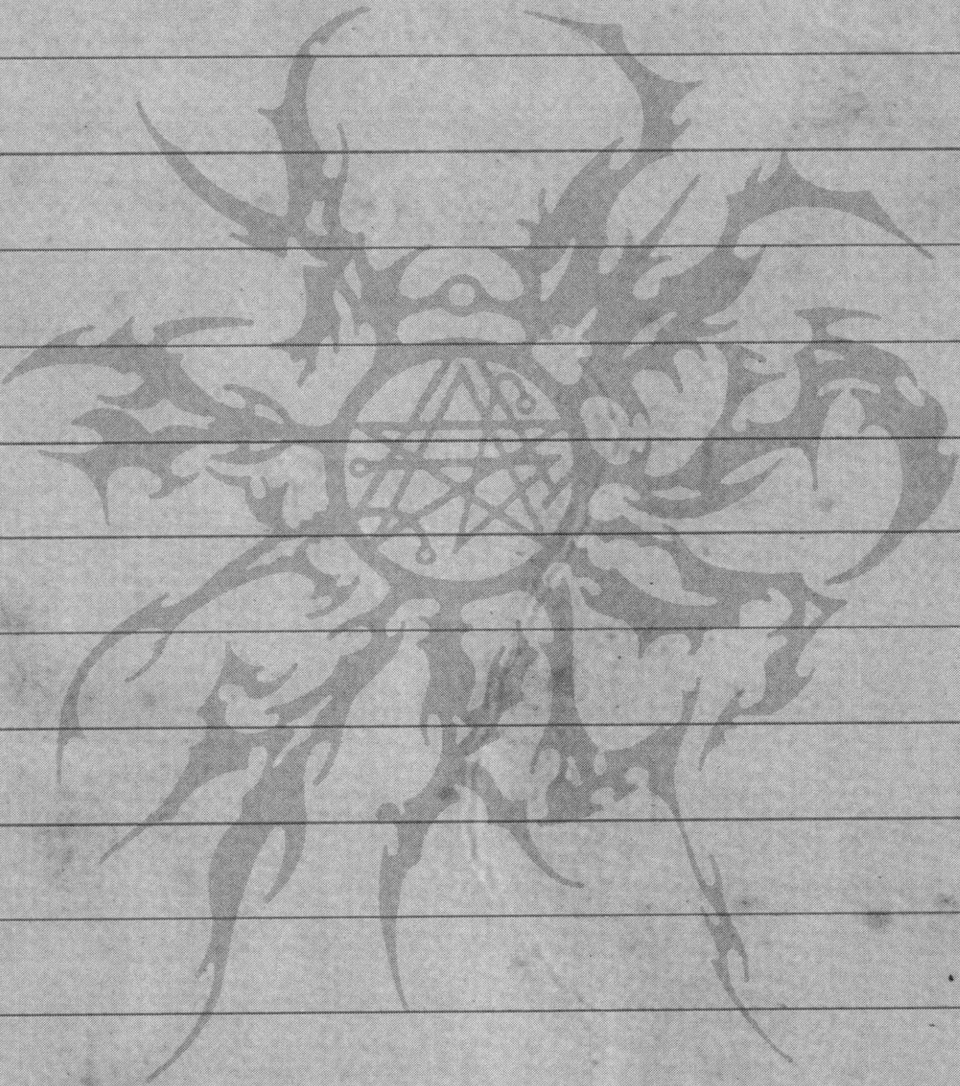

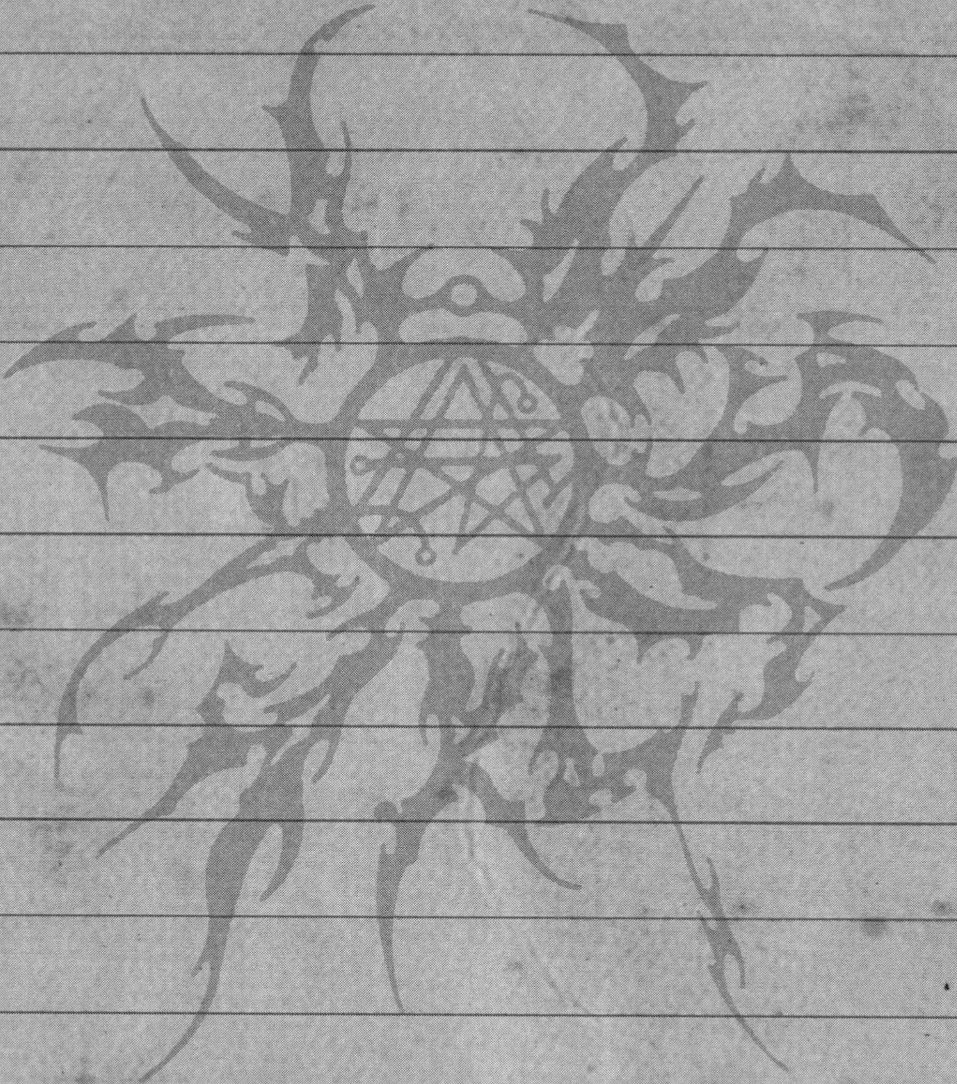

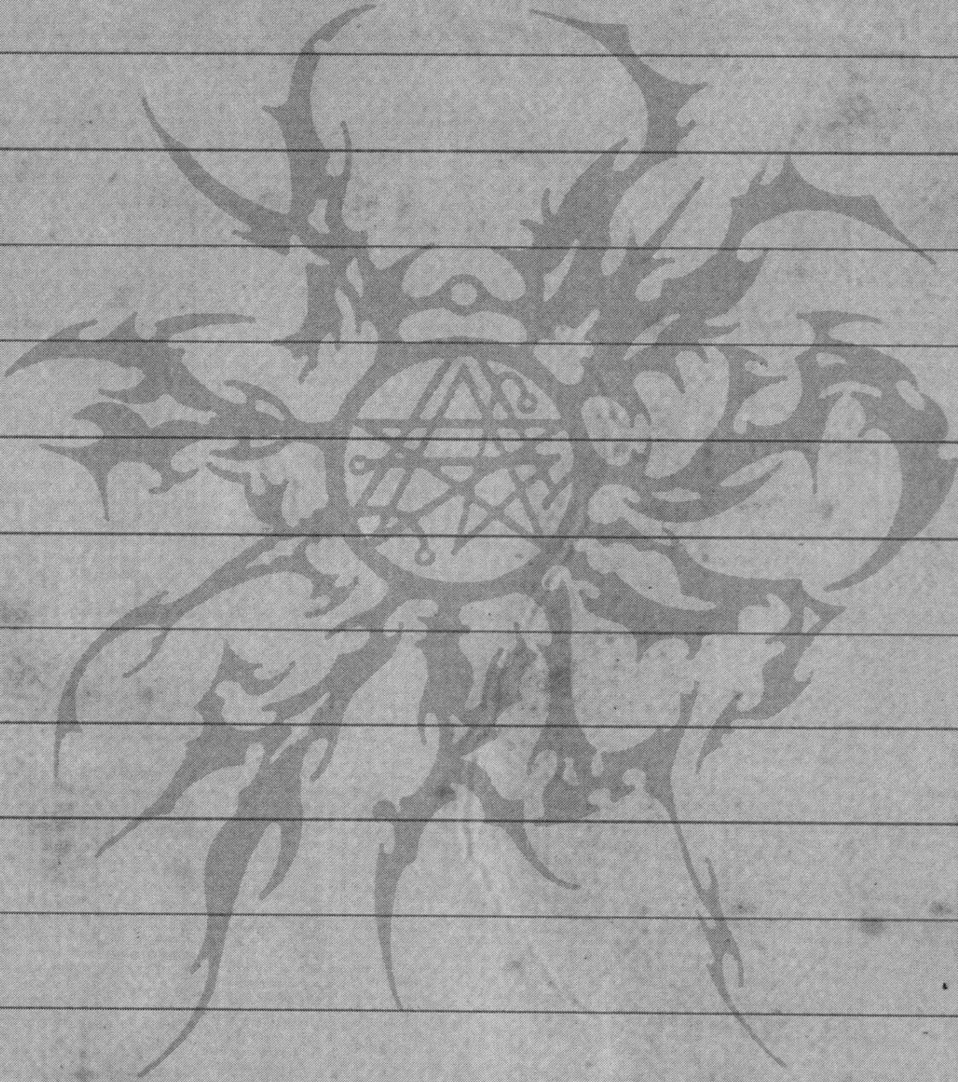

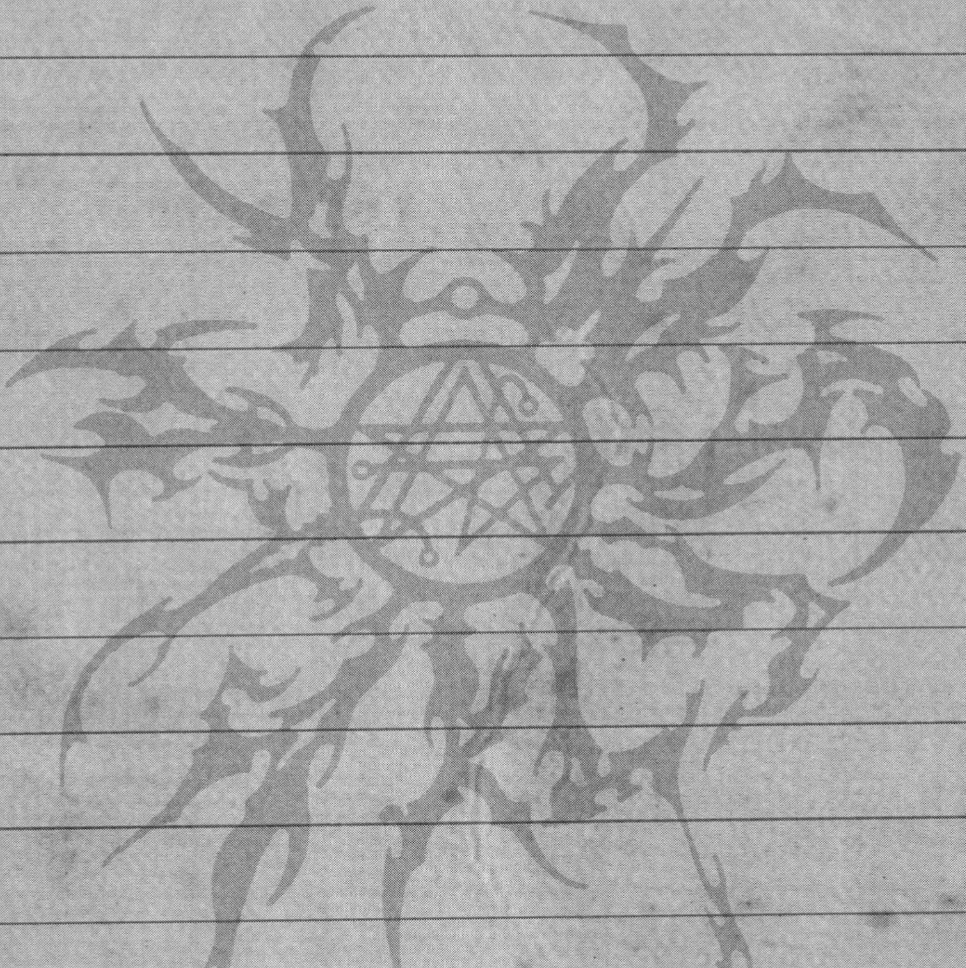

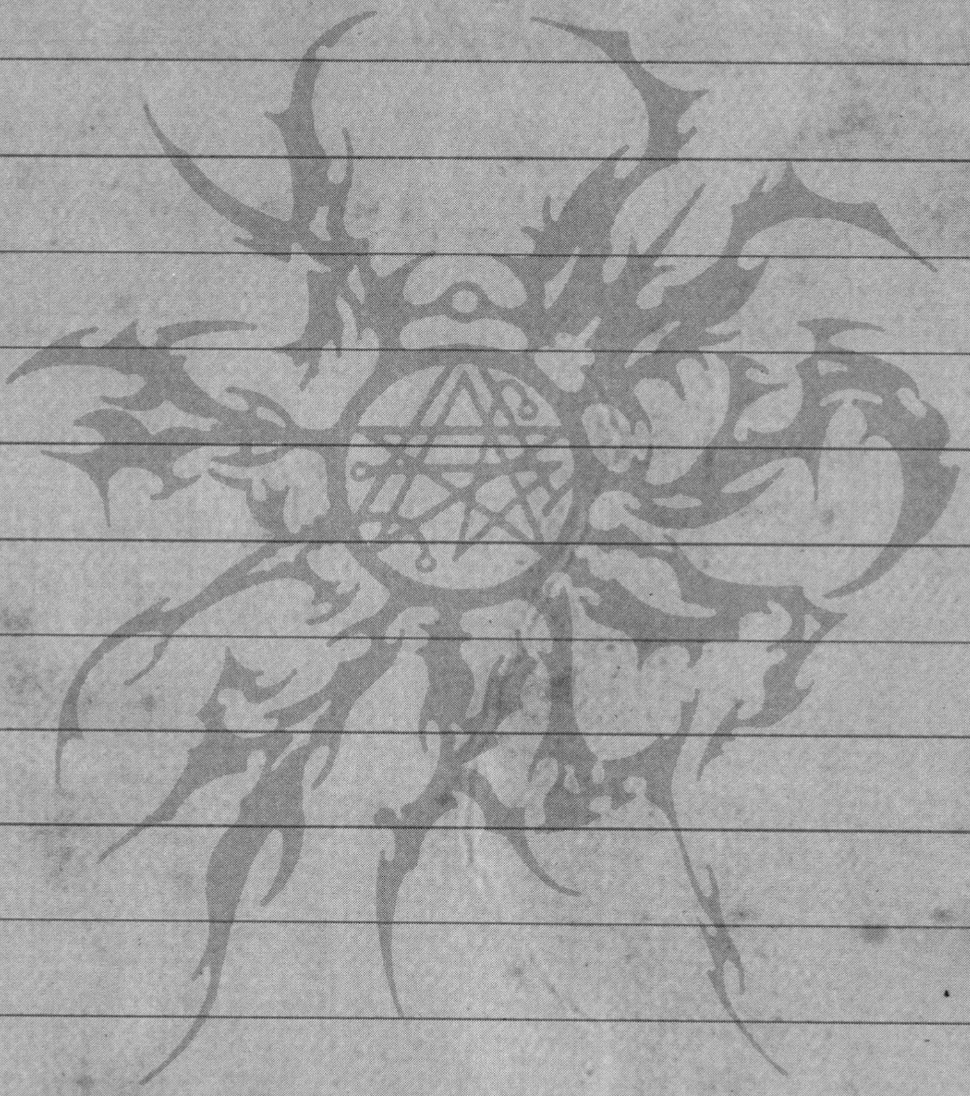

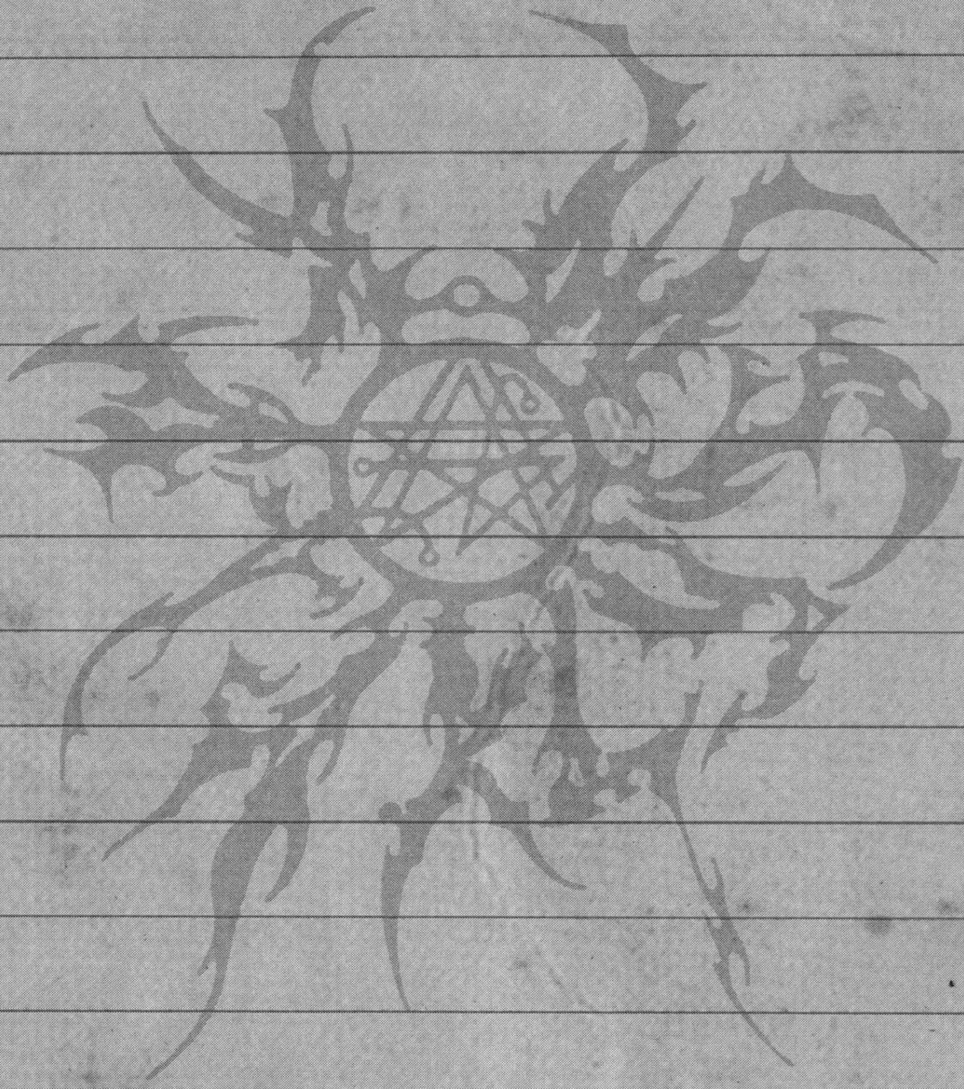

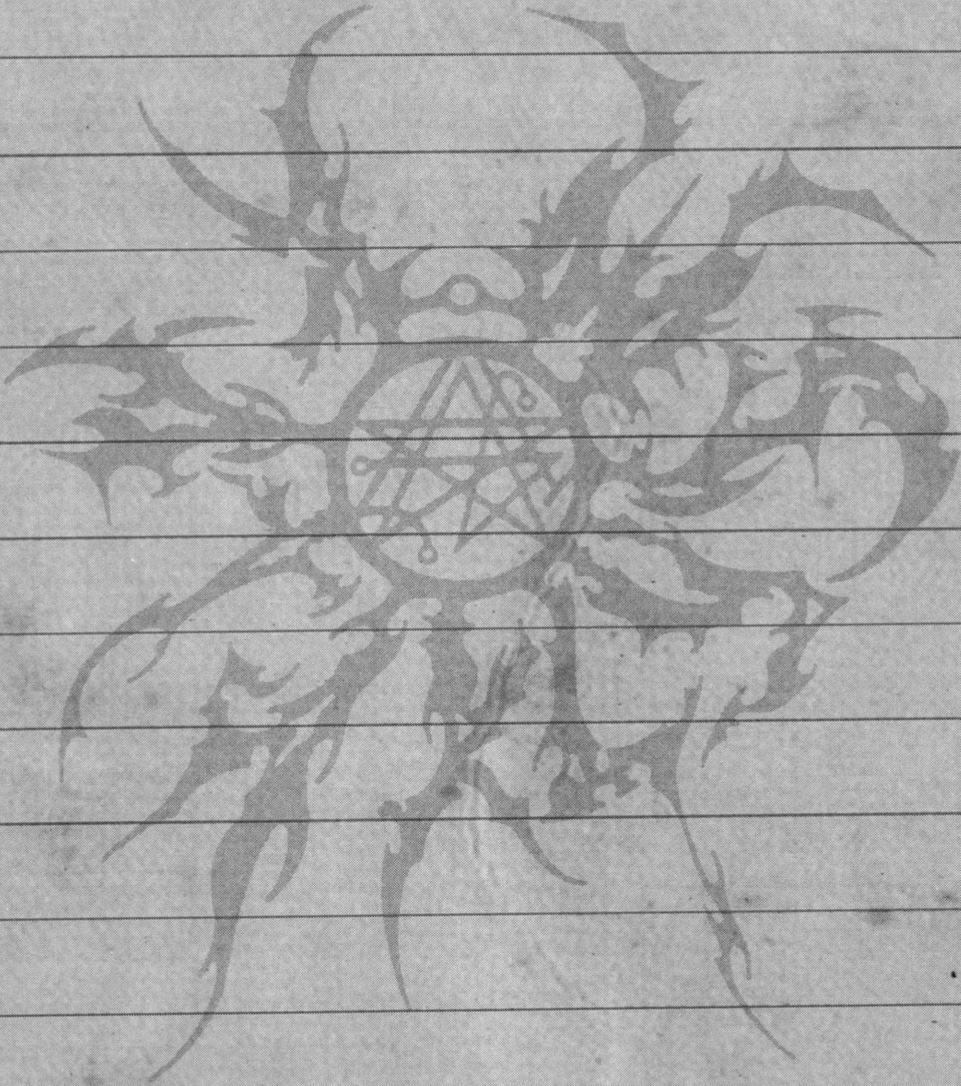

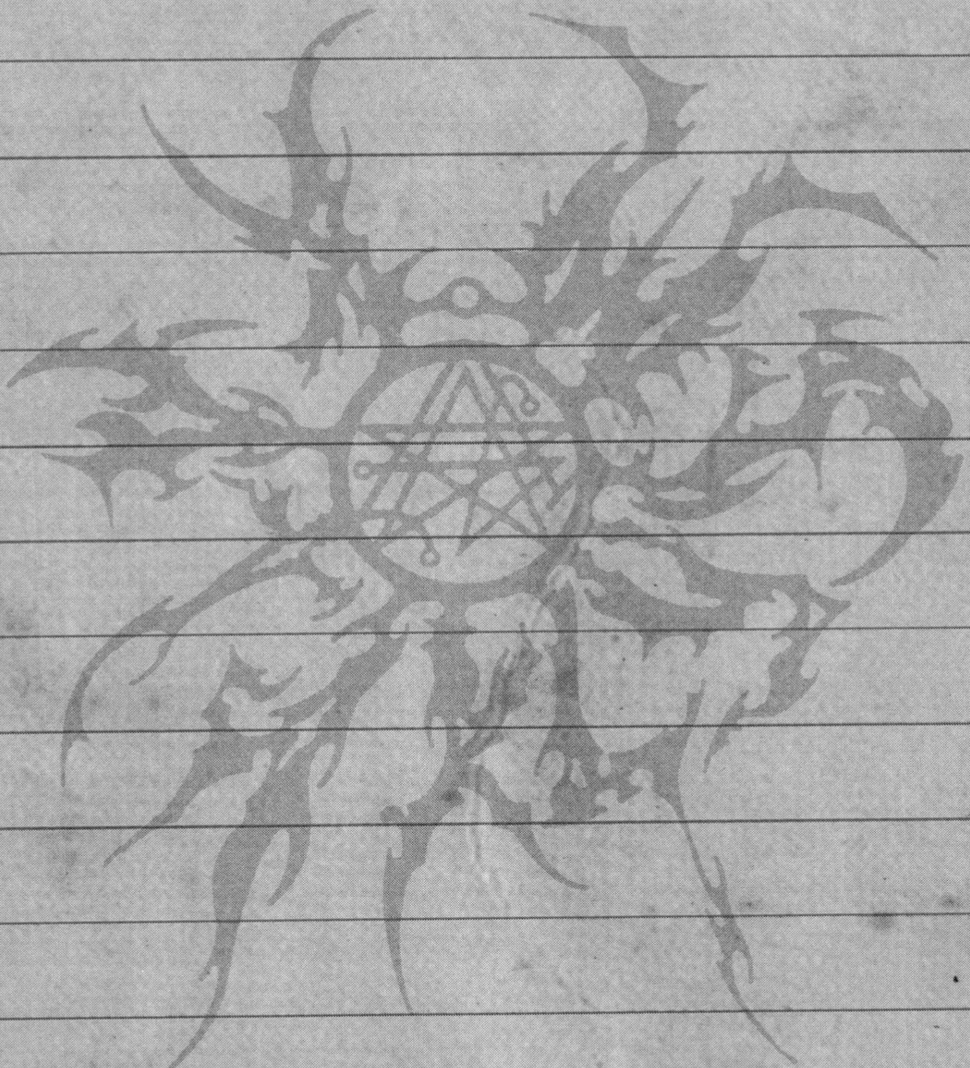

Made in the USA
Columbia, SC
20 July 2024

39047373R00074